For Christ
and His Kingdom

Christian Higher Education Canada (CHEC)

Our mission is to advance the efficiency and effectiveness of Christian higher education at member schools, including fostering institutional cooperation, and to raise public awareness of the value of Christian higher education in Canada.

www.CHECanada.ca

For Christ and His Kingdom

Inspiring a New Generation

JAMES M. HOUSTON
&
BRUCE HINDMARSH

REGENT COLLEGE PUBLISHING
Vancouver, British Columbia

For Christ and His Kingdom
Copyright © 2013 James M. Houston and Bruce Hindmarsh

Published 2013 by Regent College Publishing
for Christian Higher Education Canada (CHEC)
5800 University Boulevard, Vancouver, BC V6T 2E4 Canada
Web: www.regentpublishing.com
E-mail: info@regentpublishing.com

Regent College Publishing is an imprint of the Regent Bookstore
<www.regentbookstore.com>. Views expressed in works published
by Regent College Publishing are those of the author and do not
necessarily represent the official position of Regent College
<www.regent-college.edu>.

Library and Archives Canada Cataloguing in Publication

Houston, J. M. (James Macintosh), 1922-
    For Christ and his kingdom : inspiring a new
generation / James M. Houston and Bruce Hindmarsh ;
introduction by Justin Cooper.
    Selected addresses from the first National Forum of
CHEC on May 28-30, 2012 at King's University College,
Edmonton.
    Includes bibliographical references.
    ISBN 978-1-57383-455-1
    1. Christian universities and colleges—Canada. 2.
Christian education—Canada. 3. Church and college—
Canada. I. Hindmarsh, D. Bruce II. Christian Higher
Education Canada. National Forum. III. Title.

LC383.H68 2012   378ʼ.071   C2012-905378-3

Contents

Introduction to the 2012 CHEC National Forum Addresses

The first National Forum on Christian Higher Education took place at the King's University College in Edmonton, May 27–30, 2012, and was attended by over one hundred people, including campus leaders from twenty-two CHEC member institutions as well as other interested supporters and partners.

Sponsored by CHEC (Christian Higher Education Canada), the National Forum is an important avenue for carrying out its mission of advancing the effectiveness of Christian-centred higher education at its member schools, which include thirty-two accredited and degree granting colleges, universities and seminaries serving over 17,000 students across Canada, and raising public awareness of the value of Christian higher education in Canada.

The theme for the 2012 Forum was "For Christ and His Kingdom: Inspiring a New Generation," and throughout the plenary and breakout sessions, this theme was evident and amplified. Those in attendance sensed the Spirit's leading in the discussions throughout the three-day event. Central to setting this context were the opening and closing plenary addresses by Bruce Hindmarsh, James M. Houston Professor of Spiritual Theology, and Dr. James Houston, the Board of Governors' Professor in Spiritual Theology, both from Regent College.

Their contributions served as bookends that provided the context for the Forum and the other plenary sessions by Howard Jolly, Pastor, First Nations Community Church, Winnipeg, and Lorna Dueck, a national TV host of a current affairs program from a Christian perspective.

Dr. Hindmarsh powerfully presented the need for intellectual and spiritual integrity as essential to *paradosis*, the transmission of a living faith to the next generation. Dr. Houston's address provided a compelling case for a fulsome theological understanding of the person in Christ as intrinsic to an authentic Christian education that avoids the reductionism of secular viewpoints.

A significant highlight at the close of the Forum was the inaugural awarding of the Christian Leadership Award in Higher Education, recently established by the Board of CHEC to honour and celebrate those people who have provided outstanding examples of leadership. We were delighted to present the award to Dr. James Houston, one of the founders of Regent College in Vancouver, before he delivered his address. Our sincere congratulations and thanks to Dr. Houston for his dedicated service in higher education and beyond.

Introduction

The Forum truly met and exceeded expectations, and we thank the Lord for this blessing. Those who attended were inspired to continue the task of honouring Christ in higher education and left with a heightened sense of belonging to a national movement. The addresses of Drs. Hindmarsh and Houston were an important part of making this a reality.

CHEC would like to thank all who helped to make this first Forum a success and especially Regent College and the Institute of Religion and Culture for making these addresses available. It is our prayer that all who read them will be inspired and further strengthened in their service of Christ.

Dr. Justin Cooper
CHEC Executive Director

1

The Transmission of Living Faith

Christian Higher Education as *Paradosis*

Bruce Hindmarsh

There is a book in my library that I purchased for ten pounds sterling in the summer of 2007 on a visit to Hay-on-Wye in Wales. This is the famous town of used books on the edge of the Black Mountains, where the streets are literally lined with bookshelves (hardbacks for twenty-five pence; paperbacks for ten pence), where there are a thousand people and a million books, and where thirty-five used bookstores rub shoulders and compete for space with three ancient pubs and a ruined castle. I walked into Booth Books, the original used bookstore in the centre of the town, and noticed this early edition of a volume of sermons by John Wesley, published in 1787, four years before he died. The front boards were loose, and it had long since been separated from the other volumes in the set, but I bought it anyways, since this was the equivalent of only about sixteen Canadian dollars. Only when I got it home did I read the inscription: "These nine volumes of sermons were given by the Rev. John Wesley to my Uncle the late Rev. John King. I now give these to my Daughter, Rachel Lucinda Tause." The inscription is dated "January 30th, 1858. Thomas Tause."[1]

Now for a historian of early evangelicalism, I found it something wonderful to hold in my hand an object from the eighteenth century that was handled by John Wesley himself. Not only was it significant to me that this was once in Wesley's possession, though; it was also significant to me that he had personally *handed on* this book to one John King, who *handed it on* to his nephew Thomas, who again *handed it on* to his daughter Rachel. This inscription represents four generations of transmission of faith. John Wesley had himself encountered God in a new way as a young man at a meeting in Aldersgate Street in London in 1738, where he said he found his heart strangely warmed and that he was enabled to trust in Christ in a more per-

---

1. The handwriting is smudged and the surname "Tause" and the forename "Thomas" are difficult to make out, but this is my best conjecture. The volume is John Wesley, *Sermons on Several Occasions*, vol. 1 (London, 1787).

sonal way. It was soon thereafter that he and his brother discovered their evangelical mission to re-evangelize Britain and before long a whole generation was caught up in evangelical renewal in Britain and across the whole North Atlantic world. From that original moment of personal renewal of a living faith for John Wesley in 1738 to Rachel Lucinda Tause in 1858 is exactly 120 years, or four generations. This material book was *handed on* personally from one generation to another, and with it, evidently, a living faith.

My own career as a historian has involved research into the early evangelical movement in the eighteenth century. My last book was on conversion narrative and spiritual autobiography in the eighteenth century, and in this book I was interested in the way a whole generation came to a living, personal faith on the trailing edge of Christendom and the leading edge of modernity.[2] This was a period when so much was changing in society with the rise of science, advancing democratization, the consumer revolution, early industrialization, the first constitutional guarantees of freedom of religion, the first serious philosophical attempts to separate religion and ethics, and so on. Yet most of the population was still formally denominated as Christian, even if this mostly meant being religiously

2. Bruce Hindmarsh, *The Evangelical Conversion Narrative: Spiritual Autobiography in Early Modern England* (Oxford: Oxford University Press, 2005).

observant and maintaining a basic propriety in one's be-
haviour. So how interesting then that a whole generation
witnessed an evangelical renewal of a more personal and
active faith in Christ under these conditions. They were
converted, and they wrote about it in testimony and sang
about it in a renaissance of Christian hymnody. So I wrote
a book about conversion, and I thought often about my
own years working in evangelism with Youth for Christ in
Winnipeg, continuing to ask myself what it really means
to be converted to Christ.

Now, though, I am asking a different question in my
research. I am asking why the early evangelical revival
in the transatlantic world did not simply die out in one
generation. There was a quasi-charismatic and apocalyp-
tic phase to the early revival in the late 1730s and 1740s
where it seemed that everyone walked in a cloud of wonders. There were a number of newspapers and periodicals
from those years that died out by the end of the 1740s.
Why then didn't the whole movement die out? How did
a living faith get passed on to the next generation? Why
did evangelical religion endure through three centuries,
and, through the missionary movement, expand to five
continents?

This is not just an academic question for me. It is a
question at the front of my mind as I think about my
own children who are on their way to becoming young
adults and pray that the faith I saw alive in my parents

and grandparents will live in them also into another generation. And now that many of my graduate students at Regent College are the same age as my oldest child, I increasingly see them the same way. I stand up to teach classic texts from the living history of the church—Cassian's *Conferences* or Julian's *Shewings* or Kempis's *Imitation*—and I look out at my students and pray that the faith that lived in these previous generations of believers will live in them also.

So you can see why the inscription on my book from Hay-on-Wye is so significant for me. Perhaps we might paraphrase the inscription by Thomas Tause to his daughter on the flyleaf of my book this way: "I have been reminded of your sincere faith, Rachel, which first lived in your spiritual great-grandfather John Wesley and in your great Uncle John King and, I am persuaded, now lives in you also. For this reason I remind you to fan into flame the gift of God, which is in you." The New Testament speaks of this transmission of faith from one generation to another as *paradosis*—something handed on—or *parathecekece*—something entrusted to another—and this process has always been deeply personal. Paul speaks in this vein of the matrilineal transmission of faith in 2 Timothy 1:5, and he adopts filial language to describe his own relationship with Timothy—father and son. This transmission of living faith from one generation to another is also a vital concern throughout the Old Testament, and it is similarly personal and even filial. We see three generations appear in Psalm 78, for example, where the Psalmist writes, "I will utter dark sayings from of old: which we have heard and known, and such as *our fathers* have told us. We will not hide them from their children, but tell them to the *generation to come*, even the praises of the LORD, and his might, and his wonderful works that he hath done" (*Book of Common Prayer*, italics added). Psalm 78 proceeds to tell the narrative of how a living faith in Yahweh was passed on from the generation that witnessed the exodus down through the generations to King David, notwithstanding the recurrence of apostasy and rebellion all along the way.

John Wesley's Concern with *Paradosis*

John Wesley himself worried that the revival of vital religion he witnessed might be *res unius aetatis*, the work of one generation only. There are two places where he wrote about this. The first was in a sermon on family religion:

> What will the consequence be if . . . care be not taken of the rising generation? Will not the present revival of religion in a short time die away? Will it not be as the historian speaks of the Roman state in its infancy, *res unius aetatis*, an event that has its beginning and end within the space of one generation? Will it not be a confirmation of that melancholy remark of Luther's that "a revival of religion never lasts longer than one generation?" By a generation, (as he ex-

plains himself) he means thirty years. But, blessed be God, this remark does not hold with regard to the present instance; seeing this revival . . . has already lasted above fifty years.[3]

In this sermon, Wesley was at pains to argue that family religion was essential to *paradosis*. Wesley believed, as the Prayer Book says, that families were to be themselves "seminaries of godliness." In our modern parlance, his sermon gave practical advice on how the home could be an intentional community of spiritual formation for its members. He believed that instruction within the family about Christian formation should happen early, plainly, frequently, and patiently. This was not mere moralism, and not just a simple moral equation, though. Wesley knew that all our efforts are not enough to guarantee the transmission of faith to our children, and so he added: "While you are speaking in this, or some such manner, you should be continually lifting up your heart to God, beseeching him to open the eyes of their understanding, and to pour his light upon them. He and he alone . . . can apply your words to their hearts; without which all your labour will be in vain. But whenever the Holy Ghost teaches, there is no delay in learning."[4]

3. John Wesley, Sermon 94, "On Family Religion," §3 in *Sermons III*, ed. Albert C. Outler, vol. 3 of *The Bicentennial Edition of the Works of John Wesley* (Nashville: Abingdon, 1976–), 335.

4. Ibid., §8, 341.

So there is a hint here already that for Wesley the transmission of faith to a new generation would require focusing on Christian education. This was something he made even more plain in the annual meetings he had with his travelling preachers. In a compendium of the minutes of these meetings that he produced at the end of his life, it was clear this question was uppermost in his mind: "But what can we do for the *rising generation*?" he asked his lay preachers. "Unless we can take care of these, the present revival of religion will be *res unius aetatis*—it will last only the age of a man. Who will *labour* herein? Let him that is zealous for God and the souls of men begin *now*."[5] And then Wesley turned his attention to education. The lay preachers should preach up education and begin to focus on the young people in every Methodist society up and down the country, spending at least an hour a week wherever they could gather a group of at least ten young people. If this was to direct attention to primary Christian education (and indeed it would lead to Methodism becoming the matrix of the first Sunday schools), Wesley did not stop there. The preachers, his lieutenants in the campaign to transmit faith to another generation, would themselves require a form of higher education.

Wesley had a way of asking pointed questions in these annual meetings with his preachers. He asked them,

5. John Wesley, "The 'Large' *Minutes,* C and D (1770, 1772)," §79, in *The Methodist Societies: The Minutes of Conference*, in *Works*, 10:907.

"Why is it that the people under our care are not better?"[6] We might translate this into our own idiom by asking why the church in Canada is not stronger and healthier under the leadership of the students we have trained. Wesley summed up the conclusion of his conversation with the preachers on this point, saying there were various reasons, but the chief is "because we are not more *knowing* and more holy."[7] By this he meant that the preachers themselves needed to be better scholars ("more knowing") and needed to be better Christians ("more holy"). This was especially important to Wesley and in the 1772 edition of his *Works* he marked this section with an asterisk. When some of the preachers complained about how much reading he required of them, saying that all they really needed was the Bible, Wesley attacked this biblical literalism head on, saying it was rank enthusiasm: "If you need no book but the Bible, you are got above St. Paul." And Wesley put his money where his mouth was. To anyone who complained that he could not afford to buy books, Wesley promised to give all the books they wanted, immediately, up to the value of five pounds. That was a pretty good professional development fund, when you think that a skilled worker might not make that much working fulltime for two months, and a domestic servant might not make that much in a year. And Wesley expected them to study: an

6. Ibid., § 33, 887.
7. Ibid.

hour of Bible study in the early morning (4:00–5:00 a.m.) and the evening (5:00–6:00 p.m.), and the whole morning, from six until noon (six hours), devoted to what we might call a Christian liberal arts education. They were to work their way through the seventy books he had anthologized and published in his Christian Library (1749–55), and then they were to go on to cover the books in the four-year curriculum he had set for Kingswood School near Bristol—a formidable list of books covering all aspects of a classical education. As he wrote at the end of this curriculum, "Whoever goes carefully through this course will be a better scholar than nine out of ten of the graduates of Oxford or Cambridge."[8]

Thus, as Wesley grew old and thought about vital religion persisting into another generation, he put on a real push for Christian leaders to be well educated in the Bible and in the best tradition of the liberal arts at the time. But this was only half the equation; he also wanted Christian leaders to be more holy. And here he focused on basic Christian practice or habits. Here again, in his very direct way, he accused his preachers of being enthusiasts, which he defined as those who are "looking for the end without

8. Ibid., "The 'Large' *Minutes*, A and B (1753, 1763)," § 38, 854. Cf. *A Short Account of the School in Kingswood, Near Bristol* (Bristol, 1768), 12, and *Minutes of several conversations between the Rev. Mr. Wesley, and others. From the year 1744, to the year 1789* (London, 1791), § 29, 21.

using the means."[9] It was as if one hoped to be physically fit without ever exercising. And so he urged specific, regular, set times for prayer and fasting. The people under their care would be the better for it if their leaders were more devoted to Christ in this way.

Christian Higher Education as *Paradosis*

I have taken some space to lay out Wesley's concern for the transmission of faith to another generation and his strategic priorities, which were basic Christian formation in families and churches, and the equipping of Christian leaders for this through higher education and attention to personal spirituality. Friends, I think this is still true for us today. In the effort to pass on a living faith to a new generation, every one of us as leaders in Christian higher education in Canada today should strive to unite deep scholarship and deep devotion as a matter of first importance. This should be our strategic priority at all levels: in our own lives as Christian teachers and researchers and academic administrators, in the academic and institutional culture we foster, in formal and informal settings, in the curriculum and outside it—everywhere and always we should be concerned as a matter of first importance to strive to unite deep scholarship with deep devotion. In an address to students, B. B. Warfield said, "Sometimes we

9. Wesley, "*Minutes*, C and D," § 35, 889.

hear it said that ten minutes on your knees will give you a truer, deeper, more operative knowledge of God than ten hours over your books. 'What!' is the appropriate response, 'than ten hours over your books, on your knees?'"[10] Scholarship and devotion belong together.

Keeping scholarship and devotion together is an aspect of integrity in Christian higher education. Consider with me the both of these elements, crucial to the transmission of faith to the next generation: intellectual integrity and spiritual integrity. To emphasize the cost of failure here, I shall state these points negatively.

The Call to Intellectual Integrity

First, then, faith will surely die out within a generation without intellectual integrity. This is why Wesley demanded that his lay-preachers study widely and study deeply. Intellectual integrity is part of our Christian commitment to tell the truth. If Christian young people look back on their education only to worry that serious intellectual questions were evaded rather than faced seriously, this will of course lead to a crisis of confidence. Their education will not have survived the acid test of life in the wider world. Sectarian Christian ideology cannot sustain

10. B. B. Warfield, "The Religious Life of Theological Students," an address to the students of Princeton Theological Seminary, 4 October 1911, reprinted as a pamphlet by P&R Publishing.

a Christian very long. Sentimental pietism does not pro-
vide a sufficient foundation for life. Pragmatic activism
is a river that seeks to run on without its source. No, a
commitment to honesty in Christian higher education is a
commitment to think with our students about all that we
know about the world in the context of all that we know
of God.

Thirty-two years ago the intellectual and statesman
Charles Malik stood up to give an address at Wheaton
College at the dedication of the Billy Graham Center, and
his theme was the same as that of John Wesley: evangelism required two priorities, caring for souls and caring
for minds. But it was the latter emphasis that was long
remembered and made the greatest impression:

> The mind in its greatest and deepest reaches is not
> cared for enough. But intellectual nurture cannot
> take place apart from profound immersion for a pe-
> riod of years in the history of thought and the spirit.
> People who are in a hurry to get out of the univer-
> sity and start earning money or serving the church
> or preaching the gospel have no idea of the infinite
> value of spending years of leisure conversing with the
> greatest minds and souls of the past, ripening and
> sharpening and enlarging their powers of thinking.
> The result is that the arena of creative thinking is
> vacated and abdicated to the enemy. Who among
> evangelicals can stand up to the great secular schol-
> ars on their own terms of scholarship? Who among

evangelical scholars is quoted as a normative source by the greatest secular authorities on history or philosophy or psychology or sociology or politics? Does the evangelical mode of thinking have the slightest chance of becoming the dominant mode in the great universities of Europe and America that stamp our entire civilization with their spirit and ideas? For the sake of greater effectiveness in witnessing to Jesus Christ, as well as for their own sakes, evangelicals cannot afford to keep on living on the periphery of responsible intellectual existence.[11]

When Mark Noll published his book *The Scandal of the Evangelical Mind* (1994) fourteen years later, the theme was much the same. "The scandal of the evangelical mind," he said, "is that there is not much of an evangelical mind." Noll's report card for history and philosophy was not as bad as several other areas, but the book still made a significant impact in America and in Canada when it first came out. The journal *Books & Culture* was one of the tremendous initiatives that has been sustained as a positive response to Noll's *cri de coeur*. And there have been other voices persistently calling evangelicals to deeper scholarship in North America.

11. Charles H. Malik, "The Two Tasks," *Journal of the Evangelical Theological Society* 23 (1980): 295. The video of this presentation, 13 September 1980, is available at http://espace.wheaton.edu/bgc/video/cn003V1and2-malik.html.

This call to a thorough intellectual engagement in all areas of life remains a crucial concern for evangelical *paradosis*, since intellectual integrity is one of the integrities essential to passing on faith whole to another generation. For the apostle Paul, *paradosis* involved guarding and protecting what has been entrusted to you, and this guarding necessarily involves not only addressing critical questions but also maintaining the wholeness of the gospel for another generation. Intellectual vigour need not lead to a kind of Christian triumphalism—scoring intellectual points for our side—since that would be to fall victim to another form of reactionary dishonesty: pretending we have all the answers. Instead, the call here is to address serious questions with a faith that seeks understanding, as Anselm wrote long ago in the *Proslogion*. We go deep into our scholarship as we go deep in prayer. We do not have to have all the answers for our students to see that there is intellectual authenticity in our writing and speaking. They can tell if we are truth-seeking people, and whether we have done our homework.

So we are to love God with heart, soul, *mind*, and strength, as in Jesus' repetition of the Shema Yisrael (Mark 12:30 and parallels). Again, the great Christ hymn in Colossians 1 extols Christ as Lord, as firstborn over all creation, and firstborn from among the dead. Paul's Christ hymn brings the creation and the new creation, the world and the Church together in a great chiasm that focuses our attention on verse 17: "He is before all things, and in him all things hold together." The *ta panta*, or "all things" that hold together in Christ calls for a correspondingly robust and comprehensive intellectual life among Christ's followers that ponders deeply the "all things" over which Christ reigns supreme.

In Paul's concern for a deepening of faith in the book of Colossians, desiring that his readers be more rooted in their primary confession of Jesus Christ as Lord, he also addresses the danger of ideology, or what he calls hollow and deceptive philosophy. Here too I think we can help students develop a Christian mind in a world that has become so much more ideological than ever. It seems to me that a Foucauldian, Neo-Nietzschean elision of power and knowledge has filtered down to a popular level and shaped many of our students before they ever read a word of Foucault or Nietzsche: power and knowledge are interchangeable; there are no truths but only regimes of truth; knowledge is discourse; speech is social control; truth is what is asserted by the party in power, and so on. It is part of the air our students breathe to think in terms of the social construction of knowledge. In the humanities the cult of race, class, gender, and sexuality remains the regnant ideology likewise. Surely, this is one place to help our students develop a Christian mind. There are powerful tools of analysis here in these dominant contemporary patterns of thought, and these tools have been used prophetically by Christians, but to equate power and knowledge is, in the end, to saw off the plank you are standing on. There is no *paradosis* here. As C. S. Lewis wrote about years ago in *The Abolition of Man* (1943), the social construction of knowledge, as an ideology, leads to "men without chests." Intellect and instinct are divorced from ordered feeling. The result is a truncated anthropology, cutting off forever the possibility of cultivating an ordinate response to the world.

Intellectual integrity also requires, therefore, a transcendental, sacramental, metaphysical vision, relating the "here and now" to the "more and beyond" of our faith. We do not just package a Christian worldview and pass this on to students. There is no Christian thinking or Christian mind without a Christian metaphysic, and this is for precisely the reasons C. S. Lewis divined in the 1940s, and Augustine wrote about long ago in his great treatise *De Doctrina*. The development of a Christian mind is part of the larger response of the whole Christian person to God and his world and of the just ordering of our loves. Part of our call as Christian educators in Canada, seeking to pass on a living faith to another generation, is to help our students to love what is true, good, and beautiful in the subjects we are teaching. The neo-Aristotelian Wayne C. Booth, a leading Chicago school rhetorical critic, has written a book called *The Company We Keep: An Ethics of Fiction* (1988), in which he takes seriously the notion that books can be like friends. You may have heard the Spoonerism: "Books I have met, and people I have read." Booth believes we are shaped by the company we keep, including the books we read. There is, he says, a "trajectory of desire" in a narrative and as readers we follow this trajectory in our imagination as we follow the hopes and fears of the protagonist of a story. Booth's concern is primarily with fictional narratives, but it could also be said that there is a "trajectory of desire" in all the subjects we teach and in how we teach. There is an ethics of the told and an ethics of the telling. We and our students are therefore shaped by the company we keep.

Where do these desires, that are part of our teaching, properly terminate? I remember when my wife looked with our six-year-old son at his first science textbook and explained that he was going to learn all about God's world. He looked up at her with his wide eyes and exclaimed, "Mommy, I feel my heart going out to Jesus right now." He was always our little child mystic. That was the "spirit of joy and wonder" in all God's works that we prayed for in his baptism, and this six-year-old "trajectory of desire" is a consummation devoutly to be wished in all our education. As the Prayer Book aspires, we pray that "we may so pass through things temporal, that we finally lose not the things eternal," or again, "that among the sundry and manifold changes of the world, our hearts

may surely there be fixed, where true joys are to be found."
A Christian mind is a transcendental mind.

When I helped write our educational mission state-
ment at Regent College a few years ago, we tried to capture this in one version where we wrote:

> Our hope for students is that through their time at
> Regent College their lives will become more fully in-
> tegrated in Christ, so that their minds are filled with
> the truth of Christ, their imaginations captivated by
> the glory of Christ, and their characters formed ac-
> cording to the virtues of Christ.

These are high aspirations and beyond the reach of any
one of us on our own. This is not a package or a program,
but it is a good prayer I can pray for my students before I
teach every day.

For me, as a graduate student many years ago, my
awakening to this call to a more transcendent dimension
to study came with reading a book by the great medi-
evalist Jean Leclercq, *The Love of Learning and the Desire
for God* (1961), on the development of monastic theology
from Gregory the Great to Bernard of Clairvaux. For this
generation, what begins with the alphabet terminates in
the desire for heaven. Learning to read need not lead just
to critical debate and to *scientia*—defensible propositions;
learning to read could lead to meditation, prayer and compunction—to *sapentia* and the love of wisdom. These were

ideals too high for my maturity as a doctoral student at Oxford; I worried mostly just about academic survival. But these were worthy aspirations, and for the last twenty-two years I have been haunted, in a good sense, by this medieval vision of deep scholarship opening out into a deep devotion, and deep devotion stimulating a return to deep scholarship.

The Call to Spiritual Integrity

So far we have looked mainly at one side of the call to integrity in *paradosis*: Intellectual integrity in our times calls for faith seeking understanding, honestly and deeply; it calls for vigilance in addressing ideological challenges; and it calls for a transcendent vision as the focus of our rightly ordered desires. But then there is the other side of this call to integrity. Ten hours *on your knees* over the books, said Warfield. Wesley wanted his preachers to be both "knowing" and "*holy*." Charles Malik called for the care of the mind and the care of the soul. So, secondly, faith will surely die out within a generation without spiritual integrity. We have been hinting at this already in speaking in Augustinian terms of the right ordering of our loves, and the inherent *entelechy* in our subjects— the way, that is, that our subjects point beyond themselves and we are caught up in a trajectory of desire. I think we all know how important this is for *paradosis*, the handing on of a living faith to another generation. Rational ascendency, logical consistency, and intellectual erudition without authentic spirituality is hollow and is not playing for keeps. We are called to an integrity of word and deed, and, well, students figure out what we care about anyway. Is this intellectual enterprise something that earns one a place in the guild, that impresses a tenure committee, that scores a point for the home team? Or is this something our students can see is integral to our faith and that we would stake our lives on? Can they build their future lives on this foundation? These are vital questions when we think of education as *paradosis*.

The editors at Eerdmans have been wanting Mark Noll to write a sequel to *The Scandal of the Evangelical Mind*, which, internally, they have been calling *Son of Scandal*. I do not know whether Mark will write this book or not, but I think he would agree that there has been much progress in many fields of scholarship as evangelicals have taken seriously the call to intellectual life as a form of Christian discipleship. It may be that some of the most important work that remains to be done in Canada, as in America, concerns the building and sustaining and funding of our *institutions* of higher education so that they will be here and be healthy for another generation. It is healthy Christian institutions of higher education that can foster what the neo-Thomist Josef Pieper calls a proper sense of leisure in intellectual life—not idleness, but a freedom and detachment of the human spirit that invites contemplation and allows one to be at peace, to draw strength, and to nourish one's soul in the cultivation of ideals. He reminds us that the English word "school" derives, like the German word *Schule,* from the Greek word for leisure: *scholeœ.*[12] In most of our institutions nowadays people are run so ragged that the "human spirit" has been reduced to "human resources" for the sake of institutional survival. Healthy institutions, however, serve human ends rather than the reverse. This too is important to *paradosis.* If in Christian higher education we use up all the margins, we simply fail to allow our faculty, staff, and students to cultivate non-programmatic, non-instrumental ideals, such as those of disinterested scholarship, friendship, and prayer. Like Boaz, we must not glean to the edge of the fields lest we miss the unanticipated grace of a Ruth and Naomi.

More particularly, though, I would like to raise the question with you now as to whether the call to develop a Christian mind has eclipsed the call to develop a fully Christian spirit. What is the situation and need of this present generation today? What is the need of the hour?

Here is my present theory. The "battle for the Bible" generation was followed by the "scandal of the evangelical mind" generation. The fundamentalist generation that battled the threat of liberalism felt the need to withdraw

12. Josef Pieper, *Leisure: The Basis of Culture* (South Bend, IN: St. Augustine's Press, 1998), 3–4.

from the world and to foster a deep but narrow faith, and the children of these fundamentalists, the neo-evangelicals, reacting against this heritage, sought to re-engage intellectual and public life more responsibly.[13] So the push of one generation was in the direction of withdrawal and narrowing; the push of the next generation was in the direction of engaging and broadening. I suspect that most of our teaching faculty and administrators were part of this second generation, and I place myself here. I suspect that most of our faculty have moved during their formative years from a more narrow upbringing to a greater breadth of perspective, and they have had to make their way *in* the world, rather than *away from* it, by engaging as Christian academics with a diversity of secular non-confessional scholarship. All good. The danger comes, though, if we assume that all our students have the same needs we did in our twenties, and that what they really need *above all* is to be pushed to engage the world and to broaden their minds. Worse yet would be if we use our students as proxies to address our parent's generation with our unresolved grievances, speaking to our parents' generation rather than our children's generation with their very different needs.

13. See the excellent study by Joel Carpenter, *Revive Us Again: The Reawakening of American Fundamentalism* (New York: Oxford University Press, 1997), which may be compared with the analysis of the Canadian situation in George A. Rawlyk, ed., *Aspects of the Canadian Evangelical Experience* (Montreal and Kingston: McGill-Queens University Press, 1997).

If we assume that our students have had a basic Christian moral and spiritual formation to which we simply need to add a more sophisticated intellectual framework, we may be misconnecting. As much as our students need our finely trained minds, today they need our spiritual integrity perhaps even more. "Whatever you have learned or received or heard from me, or seen in me—put it into practice," said Paul (Phil. 4:9). Here is where life meets life.

In that old fundamentalism there was plenty of sectarianism and a reduction of ethics often to a behavioural holiness code. But there was at least a recognition that Christian formation required communities of practice and vigilance with respect to the seductiveness of the world, the flesh and the devil. And there was a desire for holy living. I am tempted to say, "Fundamentalism is dead. Long live fundamentalism!"—in the sense that the present conditions for our students' generation may require helping them to be re-grounded in basic Christian faith and practice ("the fundamentals") and in an ethic that looks different from that of our society ("separation from the world"). Here Anabaptists have taught us much. And it is telling that many of our students are attracted to the radical ideals of intentional communities and new monastic communities. Perhaps our institutions of Christian higher education in Canada should be re-imagined as intensive Christian communities, communities of basic practice, that help to shape our lives together, by God's grace, in holiness.

Please don't misunderstand me. It is not that a Christian historian can teach an inferior history class or write derivative, second-rate scholarship and make up for it with pious aspirations. For the transmission of living faith to another generation students will need to see in their teacher not just a historian but a deeply Christian person, as a whole human being, doing the work of a historian as part of a his or her larger discipleship. This also means that each one of us will need to be renewed in our own call be on our knees over our books, and that we will seek ourselves to be aligned in our scholarship in a trajectory of desire that leads to compunction. Do our students see us, in all our human condition, seeking the face of God in our scholarship? Do they see in us what in the early church was called *virtus*—a kind of moral and spiritual authority that came along with the words Christians spoke? Do they see that we recognize today our need for the grace of God? Do we offer them a trajectory of desire?

I keep an occasional journal where I write down lists of ten things for which I am grateful to God. It is especially helpful on very rainy days in Vancouver. But one day I decided to write down a list of ten people who have had the greatest influence on my life. As I looked back over the list when I was done, most of the names were former teachers. Now I know that education became my profession eventually, so that may have skewed the survey, but still, there they were on my list, the names of all those teachers: Paul Magnus at Caronport, who took time to write me a three-page letter with counsel on fund-raising when I found myself without a clue doing development work for a Christian non-profit in my twenties. Don Lewis in Vancouver, who took me for a long walk around Stanley Park to persuade me I should go do a doctorate while I was still young. John Walsh in Oxford, whose long conversations at Jesus College slowly revealed a man whose humility and Christian charity were even more remarkable than his erudition. (And I cannot think how many times he has perjured himself on my behalf in letters of reference.) With all of these teachers, there was a lot of unpaid, after-sales service. And I could go on listing other teachers. My guess is that you have your own list of teachers who have shaped your life, and that it was for you, as for me, a very personal business.

When I was a new graduate student at Regent College in the 1980s, I wrote a paper for Jim Houston, which came back with several helpful comments but also with something entirely unexpected: his phone number. He had written his phone number on the bottom of the last page of my research paper along with an invitation to come over to the house to discuss things further. I was, as they say in England, gobsmacked. Now it was not that Jim was especially efficient and organized. Over the course of my student years at Regent he lost at least two other of my research papers altogether. They vanished without a trace! But Jim was serious about forming a close relationship with me as with so many other students, and it meant much to be in his home and talk about our intellectual and spiritual concerns in the context of the whole of our lives. He continued to be my teacher long after I left Regent. In the spring of 1996, during a particularly difficult season in my life during post-doctoral work in Oxford, I sat down at a desk in the senior common room of my college and wrote a letter to Jim. I well remember the letter I received by return. Jim lovingly redirected me to see my situation differently: God was offering me a different post-doctoral education than I had planned for myself. At eighty-nine years of age, Jim continues to teach me how to live and to think, and how to suffer, and what it means to finish well. He has been my teacher, and better yet, my friend, for twenty-five years. (I shudder to think how much outstanding tuition I owe to Regent College for all those years.) Jim has lived with integrity his commitment to Christian education as personal education. And this is, for me, a tremendous example of the sort of spiritual integrity that is key to *paradosis*. It is what we read about in Deuteronomy when consideration is giving to the next generation: "These words, which I am commanding you today, shall be on your heart. You shall teach them diligently to your sons and shall talk of them when you sit in your house and when you walk by the way and when you lie down and when you rise up" (Deut. 6:6–7).

Among the desert Fathers and Mothers in Egypt in the fourth century, Christian faith was passed on in a very personal way as the word of God was received from the voice of the elder, the *geron*, in a kind of apprenticeship. As Douglas Burton-Christie has written of this movement, it was a largely oral culture making a transition to written culture, where the spoken, memorized, personalized word of God was especially cherished, and there was a great fear of reifying or "thingifying" God's dynamic word, since God's word was a word to be obeyed as a transforming word for me.[14] "Father, speak a word . . ." was how the conversation would begin. Out of this culture came the richness of the *apophthegmata*, or sayings of the desert fathers. Christie says, "The words of the holy ones were seen as participating in and continuing the discourse of the authoritative words of Scripture."[15] It was a whole culture of *paradosis*, and it was, above all, personal. It also allowed the spiritual ideals of the desert to be preserved and passed on for generations and generations.

They say that high-end, expensive automobiles need to be "hand sold," one by one, unlike the cheap cars you and I

14. Douglas Burton-Christie, *The Word in the Desert: Scripture and the Quest for Holiness in Early Christian Monasticism* (Oxford: Oxford University Press, 1992).

15. Ibid., 110.

drive. I wonder if this is not also true for the transmission of a living faith. There is no wholesaling here, and no mass marketing. It is life on life, one at a time. It is not that we will be able to be involved with all students in this way all the time, but we should each be involved with some. It is the way a living faith is passed on. I was encouraged by Susan Phillips to think of the power of even small acts of reaching out personally to students. She called it "the caring exception." Since we are not acting in our formal, paid role when we stop a student to ask how they are doing, or invite them to pray with us, they feel the force of this caring exception. We really are concerned, even when we are not on the clock.

So there two sides here to the integrity of *paradosis* in Christian higher education as we seek to hold together the call to scholarship and the call to devotion. As I was thinking and praying about what I would say to you this evening as my one opportunity to address a room full of key decision-makers and leaders in Christian higher education in Canada—those who shape the highest level of Christian catechism in this country—I asked myself what would be the one thing I would want to say. If this was my one chance to address college, seminary, and university presidents and other key leaders in Christian higher education, I decided I would say this: let us strive to unite study and prayer, learning and godliness, scholarship and devotion. There is a strange math at work here. In this equation, two minus one equals not one but zero. Intellectual life without devotion? Hollow! Spirituality without thoughtfulness? Vapid! And then again, one plus one equals not two but something more like ten or twenty. Prayer and scholarship together produce a rich harvest. What God has joined together, let no man put asunder. Why is this so important? It is a matter of first importance because this union of intellectual life and spiritual life is a form of integrity, and integrity is key to *paradosis*. Paul could say boldly to the Philippians: "Whatever you have learned or received or heard from me, or seen in me—put it into practice" (Phil. 4:9). Learned or received: there are the words and the teaching. Heard or seen: there is the life lived. Again, "Remember your leaders, who spoke the word of God to you. Consider the outcome of their way of life and imitate their faith," says the book of Hebrews, uniting words spoken with a way of life as the key to mimesis (Heb. 13:7).

Friends in Christ, fellow educators, apart from a miracle of God's grace, faith will in all likelihood die out within a generation without this sort of integrity in our homes, churches, and schools. God can save our children and our students without us, or in spite of us, but in the normal way of things, integrity of witness is crucial to the transmission of a living faith.

It might seem dramatic to put it this way, but this call to integrity is a call to martyrdom. Louis Bouyer writes about martyrdom as foundational to all Christian spirituality both genealogically and theologically.[16] As the early Christians' confession that Christ was Lord was tested by persecution unto death, it tested the integrity of their witness. Was this just words, or would they stake their lives on this, quite literally? In due course the experience of the Maccabean and Christian martyrs expanded the lexical range of the Greek word *martus* from mere "witness" to something more like its common use now in English as "witness unto death." What you are willing to die for tests what you are willing to live for. In the one of the first recorded Acts of the Martyrs in the second century, Polycarp faced the magistrate who pressed him hard, saying, "Swear the oath, and I will release thee; revile the Christ." Polycarp responded famously, "Fourscore and six years have I been His servant, and He hath done me no wrong. How then can I blaspheme my King who saved me?"[17] His life and his words were concentrated in this one moment, and this was what his life meant. His life pointed the same direction as his words. This connection between life and speech can also be seen in a modern martyr such as Dietrich Bonhoeffer. The camp doctor was moved by Bonhoeffer's execution at Flossenberg just before the end

16. Louis Bouyer, "Martyrdom," in *The Spirituality of the New Testament and the Fathers* (London: Burns & Oates, 1963), 190–210.

17. J. B. Lightfoot, *The Apostolic Fathers* (1891; repr. Whitefish, MT: Kessinger, 2003), 112.

of the war, "by the way this lovable man prayed, so devout and so certain that God heard his prayer . . . In the almost fifty years that I worked as a doctor, I have hardly ever seen a man die so entirely submissive to the will of God."[18] In martyrdom word and deed become one, and there is a perfect integrity at the end. There is no slippage here between one's public confession and the life one lives. Another way to state this is to say that God's revelation is not meant to terminate in propositions but in the bodies of women and men. A whole witness is an embodied witness, and every Christian who lays her life down in faith that God shall raise it up again bears this witness. It is in the Gospel of Luke that we see this call to martyrdom universalized as a paradigm for the whole of the Christian life and not just its end. In the pericope that follows Peter's confession of Jesus as the Christ, the son of the living God, in all three synoptic Gospels, we read Jesus' call to cross-bearing discipleship. "If anyone would come after me, he must deny himself and take up his cross and follow me." But in Luke we read, "take up his cross *daily* and follow me" (Luke 9:23 and parallels). The word "daily" here has been called the "ascetical adverb" in Luke. The integrity of witness in the martyr extends to the whole of the Christian life—every day.

18. Bruno Chenu et al., eds., *The Book of Christian Martyrs* (London: SCM, 1990), 182.

It is no longer the fashion to collect and publish death-bed narratives and confessions of pious Christians, as it was in the medieval *ars moriendi* tradition with, for example, Julian of Norwich's *Revelations*, or, in sixteenth- and seventeenth-century Anabaptism, with the *Martyr's Mirror*, or in the endless accounts in nineteenth-century magazines of evangelical home-going. The dying Christian used to get no peace as everyone strained to hear his or her last words, as when those gathered around John Wesley watched him dying and heard him sing "I'll praise my maker while I've breath," and then, a little later, whisper, "The best of all is, God is with us," and repeat this again one last time with upraised arms. The genre of evangelical deathbed narrative, or "evangelical endings" as one historian calls it, became in many instances sentimental in the later tradition, but there were still here in many instances a powerful witness to the integrity of word and deed. It all comes together at the end.

I remember a Christmas not long ago when our whole family gathered for what we all wondered might be the last time, since my father has cancer. I remember when after dinner he cleared his throat and told his six grand-children that he had something he wanted to say to them all. He quietly bore his witness to Christ before them, and spoke of his desire that they would each follow Christ, and told them that he had prayed for each of them every day of their lives, and then broke down in tears and could not say much more. In God's mercy my father is still alive, much to the surprise of his oncologists, but I can tell you that my children will never, ever, forget that dinner. It was my father's spiritual last will and testament, and none of my children will ever wonder if he really meant what he said. Students, like children, have "integrity radar" just like they have "hypocrisy radar." They know when something is authentic; they know when we are authentic. This is why the union of deep scholarship with deep devotion must be a matter of first importance in Christian higher education. It is a form of integrity. And by God's grace, it will speak loudly to the next generation as it did in Wesley's time, and even, by that same grace, to our children's children.

2

Embracing the Personal
in Christian Education

JAMES HOUSTON

Approaching ninety years old this November, and having been an academic teacher since I was twenty-five, I may be excused to give a blend of the autobiographical with the philosophical, in a lecture I have titled as "Embracing the Personal in Christian Education." For what has given me grateful satisfaction is to reflect back upon one's life as being on a continuum, like a radar beam, that has guided me all through the vicissitudes of one's biography that I call "the pursuit of the personal." Siren calls from what we may call "the professional" or "the institutional" may seek to entice us to their practical appeals, but what

I believe to be basic to being/becoming a Christian is the pursuit of "the person-in-Christ."[1] It has been very costly, and at times very complex, yet as expressive of Christian discipleship, also very simple and plain speech.

Four Educational Concerns

How Countercultural Is Christian Higher Education?

Education itself lies at the interface between "the person" and "the public." Christian educators have therefore a huge responsibility in shaping the cultural changes of Christianity, either in complying or even exaggerating the current cultural trends of society, or prophetically being counter-cultural. For example, the exaggerated importance given to professional life in the postwar Boomer generation has not usually been questioned by Christian educators but further exaggerated by them. Likewise the cultural bias toward having a "functional identity"—that what you do is more important than who you are, even as a Christian—is again furthering the secular culture rather than providing evidence of what is "true Christianity."

1. I have communicated this tension in my book *Joyous Exiles: Life in Christ on the Dangerous Edge of Things* (Downers Grove: InterVarsity Press, 2006).

How Is Activism Unquestioned?

With globalisation, and the North American messianic complex, there is no end to how busy we can be. This is very much the culture of the Boomer generation, as expressed by Susan Van Zanten in her recent book, *Joining the Mission*. Her agenda is for "mission-driven institutions," where former denominational colleges are now loosened to cooperate with other mission-driven institutions.[2] The implementation of knowledge into action is a noble educational objective, but in penetrating and challenging our secular culture, more critical thoughtfulness is required.

Why Is Scholasticism Unquestioned?

So why then, you may ask, do I also question at the other end of the educational spectrum, the sphere of scholasticism? There is the practical problem that the field of biblical academics cannot absorb all who would dearly pursue that field. So there can be two hundred Ph.Ds, in a speciality such as New Testament studies, for which there is no employment. As an early alumnus wrote me just as I was composing this reflection, "Discontented with the choice of a particular career, many students are fascinated by the new career track of Christian ministries, or of Christian academic scholarship, so they opt for them."

2. Susan Van Zanten, *Joining the Mission: A Guide for (Mainly) New College Faculty* (Grand Rapids: Eerdmans, 2011).

What better way could I choose to be a Christian than to integrate my personality trait of activism, or my bookish intellectualism of outlook, with my faith?

Is Biblical Studies the Trojan Horse of Secularism?

There is also the threat that it is precisely in the field of biblical scholarship that a Christian college can ignorantly introduce a Trojan's horse of liberal and secular scholarship, which is compromising with the secular culture. When the Scriptures are treated textually but not integrated theologically, then textual criticism will prevail in all its changing fashions. Vividly, I still remember being entertained in the faculty club of the University of Chicago, where all the mottos of the Ivy League universities are exhibited with their distinctive heraldic shields. Many of them are Christian mottos, now wholly irrelevant, the antithesis of the status quo. So my faculty friend asked me what guarantee I could give that Regent College, as we were then birthing, would not follow this secularisation process. It is a question that has haunted me ever since. Then, my only answer was that this must be a challenge for every generation, but I could not answer for the next.

Critique Reductionism in All Its Forms

Today, my response, which is the focus of this address, would be more thoughtful. The Christian, educator or just an ordinary layperson, is called to the same task, namely to denounce all forms of reductionism. If I am critiquing both activism and scholasticism as forms of reductionism, you can begin to see that the whole history of Western culture has been constantly assailed by changing, seductive ways of thinking that are also "reductionistic."

Between 1946 and 1953, I was privileged to meet almost on a monthly basis with C. S. Lewis in the home I shared with Nicholas Zernov in Oxford. I was then a young lecturer, and Zernov was the leader of the Orthodox community in England, as well as a lecturer in Russian history. So when I got married in the spring of 1953 and was leaving the partnership with Nicholas—Lewis himself was leaving Oxford to teach in Cambridge—I asked Lewis a critical question: "What would you say was your central message you were communicating through all your literary works?" Without hesitation he replied, it was "against reductionism." It was contained in the three Riddell Memorial lectures he had given at the faculty of education in Newcastle, published as *The Abolition of Man* (1943) together with his novel *Till We Have Faces* (1956). He expressed disappointment that the novel was not being accepted publicly, with an initial issue of only one thousand copies. The publisher never thought it could sell more copies. This selection illustrates what is distinctive about a true prophet. Primarily, one can only truly speak and critique from within one's own narrative of life.

Ever since he was a youth, Lewis had wanted to rewrite the Apuleius myth of Cupid and Psyche. He had trained to be a literary critic, so it was logical for him to focus upon this aspect of a changing culture; as an educator, it was logical for him to condemn the secular distortions that "scientism" now was promoting in theories of education for schoolchildren, which two young Australian educators had proposed in a school text. This was viewed by Lewis as the serious threat of secularism, to reduce the conjunction of the heavenly and the earthly onto one plane, that of materialism, in denial of the spiritual. Certainly Charles Williams' friendship with Lewis stimulated their writings to be considered "neo-Platonic," as binding the earthly with the heavenly, which is so well seen in Lewis' novel *The Great Divorce*.

What disappointed Lewis before I left him was that he considered the novel *Till We Have Faces* to be his best novel, but he sensed its message was never really understood in his lifetime. Now we appreciate that his message of the "personal" was profound. But with Lewis' use of such a range of literary genres for Christian apology, his great contribution was that Christianity requires all diverse genres for its communication. Lewis was personally attacked in the sphere of literary criticism, but those of us who were Christian teachers at Oxford were also under attack from our colleagues in philosophy, who were adopting logical positivism as their dogma. As a member of our Christian faculty, Helen Gardner pointed out in her Liddell Lectures (1956), the professionalism of scholarly criticism was becoming increasingly elite and negative.[3]

The Trajectory of the Personal

Meanwhile in the University of Auckland, E. M. Blaiklock, professor of classics, was challenged by his colleague and atheist professor of philosophy to a public debate. His address then shaped a book of essays titled *Why I am Still a Christian*.[4] It was also a response to Bertrand Russell's essay *Why I am Not a Christian*.[5] I was asked to contribute, but responded I would do so not to defend my position professionally as an academic geographer or as a historian ideas but as "a person-in-Christ" seeking faith on a personal journey. So I began by affirming,

> Rational arguments in favor of Christianity are at best partial in value. They can only skate around the circumference of the situation as it is seen and lived. I cannot wholly convince the world in mental images and languages about something I feel at

---

3. Helen Gardner, *The Business of Criticism* (Oxford: Oxford University Press, 1959), 3–4.

4. E. M. Blaiklock, ed., *Why I Am Still a Christian* (Grand Rapids: Zondervan, 1971).

5. Bertrand Russell, *Why I Am Not a Christian, and Other Related Essays on Religion and Related Subjects* (London: George Allen & Unwin, Ltd., 1957).

a much deeper level of emotion and experience. As the psalmist said: "O taste and see that the Lord is good." It is experiential rather than merely rational. As I see it, the reality and relevance of the Christian faith is its power of the personal, its insight and truth concerning human relations and purpose.

Then I went on to say, "Most of us adjust our lives so readily to the mass-minded, impersonal character of our society that we have little sense of the dimension of the personal." I concluded,

It is a risk to be a Christian, to believe in the intrinsic values of truth and righteousness, to accept the eternal dimension of Christ's revelation to man, to believe in the intrinsic value of personal relations . . . Unlike the [secular] humanist who accepts that the ultimate reality is impersonal, the Christian believes it is personal—God himself. I am still a Christian amid all the turbulence and stress of life in a great university because, increasingly, I hold this truth.[6]

What has given integration and meaning to my whole narrative more than fifty years later has been consistently living on "this trajectory of the personal" and believing it is far more valuable than just being "a professional." It has

6. James M. Houston, "A God-Centered Personality," in *Why I Am Still a Christian*, 83–84, 93.

been a costly journey that not even fellow Christians have understood.

So I agree with Parker Palmer in his significant book *The Courage to Teach* that it is the inner character of the teacher that counts more than all the changes to and re-designs of our curriculum of education. In his book, he explores "the heart of the teacher" as having identity and integrity so that beyond the superficial issues raised by the questions of "what," "how," or even "why" we teach, we ask "who" we teach.[7] As Lord Bullock, Master of St. Catherine's College, where I did some teaching, used to tell us, "It is an immature tutor whose primary interest is 'the subject'; rather it is the mature teacher whose primary interest is the pupil."

For the basic thrust of education, *educere*, is to evoke wonder and to enlarge horizons, which new insights and new discoveries certainly help us to do.[8] In a tripartite balance we should be engaged in the harmony of research, teaching, and personal engagement. Placing one's identity in a profession or in a career is fatal to this balance; it requires a much broader basis of seeking to become a richer person in all of one's relations, especially for Christians,

7. Parker J. Palmer, *The Courage to Teach: Exploring the Inner Landscape of a Teacher's Life* (San Francisco: Jossey-Bass, 1998), 1–7.

8. Andrew Delbanco, *College: What It Was, Is, and Should Be* (Princeton and Oxford: Princeton University Press, 2012), 3.

who seek to be "in Christ." This goes then much further than May Sarton's poem:

> Now I become myself. It's taken
> Time, many years and places;
> I have been dissolved and shaken
> Worn other people's faces.[9]

This is grounded upon Catholic morality of natural law and Aristotelian human inner potency with the "true self." But the evangelical giftedness of being found "in Christ" is much more—as E. Stanley Jones so persuasively argues, it is "the only way to live."[10] It is what Calvin so persuasively and simply asserts as "participation in Christ" in his *Institutes*.[11] Many wanted to accept Jesus as a great Teacher, but while many teach great things, only Jesus Christ can impart to us eternal life. So too for the Christian teacher, our teaching, whatever it is, should also be life-giving by the presence we have in the lecture hall or seminar room, regardless of whether we are teaching science or the humanities.

Even a good secular teacher knows that good teaching cannot be reduced to a technique; it comes from within the character of the teacher. More than merely correcting

9. Quoted by Palmer, *Courage to Teach*, 9.

10. E. Stanley Jones, *In Christ* (Nashville: Abingdon, 1961).

11. Julie Canlis, *Calvin's Ladder: A Spiritual Theology of Ascent and Ascension* (Grand Rapids: Eerdmans, 2010).

examination papers of her students, she is exemplifying in both "doing and being," what teacher and student share together, with the whole class or laboratory audience.

Classical education is modeled on the role of the *paideia*, the mentor friend.[12] Because of the tutorial system I was privileged to participate in for twenty-three years, this has certainly been my own life's inheritance. Pierre Hadot has so eloquently described classical education as "philosophy as a way of life." Philosophical discourse is then not the beginning but the conclusion of a way of living. "The philosophical school" thus corresponds above all to the choice of a certain way of life, a personal choice and decision that is never made in solitude. For it can only be practised in a community, a "school." "*Theoria*" was not abstract theory but a life dedicated to being a personal thinker. Plato and his friends in the Academy shared a certain conception of knowledge as "the training of human beings, as the slow and difficult education of the character, as the harmonious development of the entire human person, and finally as a way of life."[13]

In contrast, a "sophist" was a professional teacher, a salesman of knowledge, who taught the art of persua-

12. James M. Houston, *The Disciple: Following the True Mentor* (Colorado Springs: Cook, 2009).

13. Pierre Hadot, *What Is Ancient Philosophy?*, trans. Michael Chase (Cambridge, MA: Belknap Press of Harvard University Press, 2002), 64.

sive discourse to seduce his audience with words, not life. Sophists never established communities. This was "the false wisdom" the apostle condemns in his Corinthian epistles—the sophist teachers were strongly present in Corinth.[14] Alas, it is this Sophist inheritance we now have in our technological society, not the Socratic/Aristotelian. In the latter, the curriculum (*curere*), or course, involved the student and *paideia*/mentor/coach running track around the gymnasium together, engaged in the task of "finishing the race" as expressive of "a way of being"—the pursuit of excellence, or *arēte*.

John Henry Newman's Idea of a University

When I was invited in 1966 to consider creating a Christian institution of higher education in Vancouver, my thoughts turned to Newman's classic *The Idea of a University*, consisting of ten lectures he gave in Dublin in 1852. British Parliament passed a bill in 1845 to create three new "Queen's colleges" in Belfast, Cork, and Limerick. After becoming a Roman Catholic in 1845, John Henry Newman (1801–90) was asked by the Roman Catholic Primate of Ireland to give advice about founding a Catholic university in Ireland. In 1852, as rector and president elect, he gave ten lectures, which became the substance of

14. Bruce W. Winter, *Philo and Paul among the Sophists*, 2nd ed. (Grand Rapids: Eerdmans, 2002).

his book. The prime minister, Robert Peel, as an Anglican, would never have allowed this Catholic-Protestant union of what later became three universities in Ireland to have occurred in England. Indeed, the popular objection to the new University of London was that it was not going to include theology in its teaching, an issue it later compromised on. Secularisation was then in the beginnings of its tidal change, which Matthew Arnold would later to mourn in his poem "Dover Beach."

Ironically, Newman's radical change from Anglican clergyman to Roman Catholic priesthood and then to cardinal provided a projection of Oxford education into the rigidity of the Catholic priesthood. As if he were still a fellow of Oriel College and the famous preacher of St. Mary's church, he tried to create an academic community that was not like the impending secularised university education.[15]

He made five points. Firstly, a university should not be solely a research institution, for the primary purpose of Christian higher education should be the shaping of the minds and lives of young people. Secondly, such a university community should not be a board of examiners for certifying that young people have acquired the minimum education. As Newman put it, "A set of examiners with no opinions which they dare profess, and with no common

15. John Henry Newman, *The Idea of a University* (Notre Dame: University of Notre Dame Press, 1982), viii–ix.

principles, who are teaching or questioning a set of youths who do not know them, and do not know each other, on a large number of subjects, different in kind and connected by no wide philosophy—that is not a university."[16] Thirdly, a university should not be content with handing out information; it must engage in developing lifelong habits of learning, the capacity for wise judgments, and the sound shaping of character. (The administrative skills learned in a classical education at Oxbridge were indeed the sinews that ensured the rise of the British Empire in the Victorian era, which still influences the civil service of India.) Fourthly, argued Newman, a university should instill wisdom—education is not merely encyclopedic, a repository of information. It is not so much a place for "accomplishments" but a community for the enlargement of the mind and heart in Christian faith.

So Newman concludes with a hymn of praise for his idealistic vision of higher education, describing five "almost" utopian traits: it is *almost* prophetic in its knowledge of history; it is *almost* heart-searching from its knowledge of human nature; it is *almost* supernaturally charitable in its freedom from littleness and prejudice; it is *almost* the repose of faith, because nothing can startle it; it is *almost* the beauty and harmony of heavenly contemplation, so

16. Owen Chadwick, *Newman: A Short Introduction* (Cambridge: Cambridge University Press, 2010),131.

intimate is it with the eternal order of things and the music of the spheres."[17]

Just over a century later, I was a professional colleague of Gilbert White, then professor of geography at the University of Chicago who spent a sabbatical year at my college in Oxford. He was an advisor to the board of regents of the University of California, which was expanding its campuses in growing communities in California. He had special interest in the campus of Santa Barbara, which was dedicated to imitating the collegial character of Oxford. So he asked me whether he could put my candidature forward to head the school of geography at this new university campus. But my mind then was too full of Newman's *Idea of a University*, which I expressed to the search committee. That was not the "Oxford" now being imitated at Santa Barbara, but it prepared me a few years later for Regent College in Vancouver.

Newman's fatal flaw that I had not yet realised was that Christianity is not a branch of knowledge; it is a way of life. Socrates and Aristotle would have understood this more sympathetically, as we must still do.

17. Ibid., 55, 123–24.

A Christian *Apologia* for Becoming Personal as the Christian Way of Life

What I now communicate in the second half of my address is an *apologia* for the continued presence of Christianity in secular academia. It can only be in living and then in teaching *personally*. Ironically, it may be through the threat of the increase of dementias of various kinds—resulting from medical advances being made to increase the aging of the society—that medical ethicists are now beginning to question the hyper-cognitive expressions of identity we have inherited from the Enlightenment.[18]

Beginning with Descartes' "I think, therefore I am," John Locke then defined the self as "a thinking, intelligent Being, that has reason and reflection, and can consider it self as it self, the same thinking thing in different times and places."[19] Later, David Hume in his *Treatise of Human Nature* identifies an individual *with* a mind rather than with a sort of being that *has* a mind. He considers a self as nothing more than a bundle of perceptions.[20] It creates an extremely strange predicament for gerontologists that a

18. Julian C. Hughes, Stephen J. Louw, and Steven R. Sabat, *Dementia, Mind, Meaning, and the Person* (Oxford: Oxford University Press, 2009).

19. John Locke, *Essay Concerning Human Understanding*, ed. P. H. Nidditch (Oxford: Clarendon, 1975), 335.

20. David Hume, *A Treatise of Human Nature*, ed. L. A. Selby-Biggs and P. H. Nidditch (Oxford: Clarendon, 1978), 252.

term such as "person" refers to *something*, yet we are unsure what that kind of *thing* refers to. A medical patient also need to be treated as more truly a "person."

As I interpret it, there have been four major attempts to address the reductionism concerning "the personal self" since the impact of the Enlightenment.

Johann Georg Hamann's Critique of the Enlightenment

The first voice is that of Johann Georg Hamann (1730–88), a friend of Immanuel Kant. They lived together in Koenigsburg. He was the brightest intellect of his time, wrote Goethe later. Isaiah Berlin appraised Hamann as "the first out-and-out opponent of the French Enlightenment . . . that in the end engulfed all of European culture."[21] As a humble journalist who earned his keep as an employee of the port's custom office, he described his writings as "flying leaves/leaflets" of no literary consequence unlike the big philosophical handbooks of his peers Kant, Lessing, Hegel, and Herder. His approach is that of *kenosis*, following the New Testament's emphasis of the "self-emptying" Son of God.[22] So the word, like the

21. Isaiah Berlin, *Magus of the North: J. G. Hamann and the Origin of Modern Limitationalism* (London: Fontana, 1994), xv, 4, 22, 71, 107. As a secular Jew, Berlin can only describe such New Testament "kenotic knowledge" as "limitationalism." For without the mystery of the Incarnation, *kenosis* is meaningless.

22. J. G. Hamann, *Writings on Philosophy and Language*, ed. Kenneth Haynes (Cambridge: Cambridge University Press, 2009), xiii.

wind, "blows where it will" (John 3:8). In reflecting upon Job's sense of transience, a human life is like a leaf blown in the wind; it "lives a few days, full of trouble, comes up like a flower and withers, flees like a shadow and does not last" (Job 14:1). Yet this human lightweight is encountered by the eternal God, so Job in astonishment and awe asks, "Do you fix your eyes on such a one that you bring me into judgment with you?" (Job 14:3). Psalm 8:4 wonders, "What am I that you remember me in this way," bestowing reason on me? In contrast, Hamann's academic contemporaries were domesticating their mere concept of a god as a necessary postulate for their own logical systems of philosophy.

Hamann's starting point was that "the fear of the Lord is the beginning of wisdom . . . to fear and love him." Evangelical wisdom is the consequence of such a "kenotic life" lived by the gospel. Further, argues Hamann, when humanity encounters the Creator, humanity faces judgment—the same judgment that separated light from darkness, the ocean depth of chaos from the bounded land of fecundity. Hamann had been confronted with this awareness personally on a visit to London in 1758, which led to his profound conversion. In reading his Bible, he found it as "a descent into the hell of self-knowledge"[23]—the *krites* ("criticism") he encountered was that the God of

23. Oswald Bayer, *A Contemporary in Dissent: Johann Georg Hamann as a Radical Enlightener* (Grand Rapids: Eerdmans, 2012), 6, 39.

the Bible became the Author of his own life as well as of the history of the world. It was thus as a follower of the heavenly Critic that Hamann's life was called to be a critic of his contemporaries' vaunted boast of the illumination of the Enlightenment.

As Aristotle had used "criticism" in his *Politics*, it was the quality of a citizen of the *polis* to fully participate in its judicial functions in *krisis* and in office (*arche*). In contrast, the small farmers and slaves were mere onlookers and backbenders. Hamann was probably the first reader of Kant's *Critique of Pure Reason*, which challenged him to become a "meta-critic" in negating Kant's fundamental premises.[24] For in their true relationships, biblical people were for Hamann those whose relational lives combined dependence and autonomy, authority and criticism, the temporal and the eternal, the cross and the eschaton—for Christ is both Lord of all and Servant of all. Indeed such "people" are free lords of all things and subject to none, yet dutiful servants of all things and subject to everyone.

In all these personal paradoxes, Hamann could confess, "I do not know myself, but God understands me!"[25] This was the exclamation of Sancho Panza, the simple squire of Don Quixote, and it became the basis of Hamann's own critical pen. He was attacking the windmills of monarchic

24. Robert Alan Sparling, *Johann Georg Hamann and the Enlightenment Project* (Toronto: University of Toronto Press, 2011), 57.

25. Bayer, *Contemporary in Dissent*, 40, 42, 62.

reason with their imperial desire to capture the wind, or to assume human reason can capture the mind of God. With passion he attacked all forms of reductionism as expressed by Descartes, Kant, and Hegel. In his confession, *Thoughts about My Life Story*, he develops his thoughts very much in tune to what Bonhoeffer was later to formulate about himself:

> Who am I really, what others say about me?
> Or am I only what I myself know of myself?
> Who am I? They mock me, these lonely questions
>   of mine.
> Whoever I am, Thou knowest, O God, I am Thine![26]

We are all tossed between individuality (*ipse*) and sociality (*idem*), with a loss of self in the sea of "others" or a loss of community in the abyss of "me." In the Pietist culture that spawned this agony, Kant and Hegel were swept into the ocean of idealism while Herder in his discourse on language and Schleiermacher in his discourse on religion go underground into subjectivism. Hamann alone sustained the dialectic within the human as well as between the human and the divine by living according to the Bible. A frequent petition of Hamann was from Psalm 90:12: "So teach us to number our days that we may gain a wise heart." In his *Biblical Meditations*, he prays, "Lord,

26. Facsimile copy in Eric Metaxas, *Bonhoeffer* (Nashville: Thomas Nelson, 2010), 464.

Thy Word makes us wise, even if it teaches nothing more than to number our days. What a nothingness, mere smoke, a spiritual nothingness they are in our eyes when reason numbers them! What a fullness, what a treasure, what an eternity when faith numbers them. Lord, teach me to number my days that I may apply thy Word to illumine our spirit. All is a labyrinth and disorder when we try to look for ourselves."[27] The density of Hamann's voice still carries a powerful witness to our ongoing need today for theological anthropology.

Soren Kierkegaard's Attack against Cultural Nomialism

The second response to Enlightenment reductionism is Søren Kierkegaard (1811–55), who was influenced by Hamann more than scholars have appreciated. Ironically, he shares Hamann's "floating leaves" with his own "philosophical crumbs" of Socratic dialogue. For he too is not "serving the system" with all its parades of rationalistic "-isms" that assume "my system of reasoning is the only way of thinking"; no, Kierkegaard is iconoclastic in parody of all "systems."[28] But bread crumbs feed our bodies (as in the parable of Jesus feeding the five thousand). Even breadcrumbs have nourishing value, while sophistry has none. "The only thing I can do for thought, I who can-

27. Bayer, *Contemporary in Dissent*, 198.
28. Søren Kierkegaard, *Reflections and Philosophical Crumbs*, trans. M. G. Piety (Oxford: Oxford University Press, 2001), xvi–xvii.

not offer erudition, hardly the one drachma course [of the poor widow who offered her all] . . . I have only my life, which I offer as soon as a difficulty appears." Raising the Socratic question of how the truth can be taught, Kierkegaard argues that the teacher must bring it to the student—and not just the truth but the condition for understanding it. But the teacher cannot transform the learner to make this possible if the learner, as a slave to sin, needs inner liberation. The teacher can assess the situation, but then the teacher is more of a judge than a teacher capable of freeing the learner to become a new person. So Kierkegaard proceeds in a lyrical essay to argue for God being both our Teacher and Saviour who alone can love us and free us from the bondage of sin and our inability to receive and live by the truth. So in the veiled language of incarnation, Kierkegaard is arguing how learner and Teacher are bound in a union of revealing and of being able to learn the truth of God.[29]

What challenged Kierkegaard was the state of Christendom in Denmark, in which the state church baptised every child born in the nation so that all were legally "Christians." In his work *The Practice of Christianity* Kierkegaard focuses upon three things that deadens the nation's religious life: (1) its intellectualism—"the direct assent to a sum of doctrines"; (2) its formalism—"battalions upon battalions of unbelieving believers"; and (3) its

29. Ibid., 92–173.

phariseeism—a herd of hypocritical clergy that ignores the Christianity they are hired to preach.[30] As Hamann was challenged by idealism, Kierkegaard was challenged by nominalism. This was not just a struggle between orthodoxy and heterodoxy but of orthopraxis, of how the truth is to be lived personally.

Kiekegaard was not just contending with the outward culture but also with unrealistic relations in his private life. As the child of an old, melancholic yet strictly pious father, an inner inconsistency challenged him immensely. In his love for the sixteen-year-old Regine, he felt he could not share the inner secrets of his melancholy, so he perceived his marriage would be based upon a lie. For this reason he broke off the engagement.

Interpreted as the originator of existentialism, Kierkegaard is far more in pursuit of the personal. To be a genuine human being, a "person," was his central concern. This requires transcending oneself as "aesthetic"—as life lived for the moment—or as "ethical"—a moral life of choice, struggle, and determination. Then one must also be "religious," in the sense of living a life that it is fully actualised before God, to see onself as a sinner in need of a Saviour.[31] Then the individual can never see him- or

30. Charles E. Moore, ed., *Provocations: Spiritual Writings of Kierkegaard* (Maryknoll, NY: Orbis, 2010), xi.

31. James M. Houston, *The Mentored Life: From Individualism to Personhood* (Vancouver: Regent College Publishing, 2011).

herself as self-sufficient but rather in need of transformation by God. The Christian person therefore has a very different existence from the rest of humanity. It is to be a unique self, standing accountable to God alone, integrated to serve God, and free to decide all issues in the sight of God.

In the constant sequence of ideologies, Kierkegaard is resolute that every "idea" has to come into "existence" to be true. "Most systematizers," he notes (echoing a similar analogy of Hamann's), "stand in the same relation to their systems as a man who builds a great castle and lives in an adjoining shack; they do not live in their great systematic structure." Little did Kierkegaard know how true his words anticipated the ideological shacks where Marx, Stalin, Hitler, and their followers were later to take shelter.

"The single individual" is Kierkegaard's key to the inwardness of faith, which the true Christian person should possess. First, it means to stand alone before God in accountability and unique and naked awareness of God. Second, it means being an integrated self ordered by a single purpose. For "purity of heart is to will one thing." Third, an individual is a responsible self who in freedom gives account of him- or herself. Finally, to be a genuine human being is to exist as a unique self, standing out of the crowd. So when we claim to embrace the person in Christian education, we may well ask, How clearly do we claim and live by the principles depicted by Søren Kierkegaard?

Personalist Voices against the Ideologies of the Twentieth Century

Third, there were a number of thinkers who reacted against socialist reductions of "the person" in the twentieth century. Fyodor Dostoyevsky was the nineteenth-century Russian prophet who spoke against the impending system of socialism in Russia; he was prescient about its destruction of the person. In his great novel *The Brothers Karamazov*, Ivan the main character represents the systematizer that Kierkegaard despised or the Kantian moralist that Hamann attacked. Ivan gives the great line, "In my view, it is the neighbours that one can't possibly love, but only perhaps those who live far away. . . . To love a man, it is necessary that he should be hidden, for as soon as he shows his face, love is gone."[32] Since Ivan as a child had never known a father's love, now as an adult, "love" continued to remain an abstraction. What was true of European socialism is still true of American liberalism, both forms of reduction that abstract the human condition to statistics and ideologies. John Haidt is still struggling with

---

32. Fyodor Dostoyevsky, *The Brothers Karamazov*, trans. David Magarshack (London: Penguin, 1982), 276.

this disillusioning awareness in his recent work *The Righteous Mind.*[33]

In his novel *The Stranger*, Albert Camus depicts the mind of the alienated individual through his chilling character Merseult's senseless murder of a nameless "other" labeled "the Arab." Indeed, secular existentialism and Marxism after it have portrayed a much more complex quest for "the person" in the twentieth century than we can hope to even outline. In succession, Martin Buber, John Macmurray, Gabriel Marcel, Immanuel Mounier, Michael Polanyi, Paul Ricoeur, and John Zizoulas have all made profound contributions to eliminate reductionism in pursuit of the personal.

I was fortunate to be on the fringe of this incipient renaissance as a student at Edinburgh, where John Macmurray taught, then as a neighbour of Michael Polanyi in Oxford, and then as a family friend of T. F. and James Torrance, who were greatly influenced by Macmurray and Polanyi. When I arrived in Vancouver for the beginning of Regent College, T. F. Torrance gave me all his lecture handouts on his courses in systematic theology. The report to the council of churches in Britain intended as a wakeup call for the recovery of "the forgotten Trinity" in the renewal of Trinitarian theology was chaired by my long-time colleague James Torrance. Colin Gunton was

33. John Haidt, *The Righteous Mind: Why Good People Are Divided by Politics and Religion* (New York: Pantheon, 2012).

a student at Hertford College when I was a fellow there in the 1960s. He gave a brilliant critique of the Enlightenment (although he confessed personally to me that Hertford gave him a poor theological education, which he thought still handicapped him years later!). Alan Torrance, now another family friend, is seeking the establishment of an academic institute for the pursuit of biblical anthropology.[34]

In celebrating this inauguration of CHEC, I can think of no higher mission for Christian higher education in Canada than this mandate of "embracing the personal in Christian education." As our outline has demonstrated, we are not just being more sociably friendly. We are facing the rigours of a serious intellectual endeavour whenever we challenge the reductionism of mind and spirit, whether we call it "liberal" or "secular." As Polanyi begins his small work *The Study of Man*, "Man's capacity to think is his most outstanding attribute. Whoever speaks of man will therefore have to speak at some stage of human knowledge."[35] Yet as soon as the knower is engaged in pursuit of further knowledge, "he catches himself red-handed in the act of upholding *his* knowledge." "Personal knowledge," by contrast, is "participatory knowledge," where

34. Alan J. Torrance, *Persons in Communion: Trinitarian Description and Human Participation* (Edinburgh: T&T Clark, 1996).

35. Michael Polanyi, *The Study of Man* (London: Routledge & Kegan Paul, 1959), 11.

subject and object are never detached. This is what he calls "tacit knowledge,"[36] or what Kitty Muggeridge more simply called at the end of her life "gazing upon truth."[37] It implies, says Polanyi, an understanding, an indwelling, and an appreciation that are closely interwoven. By the act of the appreciation of another person's mind, we enter into a fellowship with the other thinker and acknowledge that we share the same firmament of obligations. As the biblical narrative unfolds, human stewardship of the whole creation is a sacred trust to "name it" and to be stewards over it. For as Polanyi observes, "We on this earth are the only bearers of thought in the universe."[38] Therefore, while universities should appropriately train doctors, lawyers, and teachers for the professional life of contemporary society, they have a far more solemn responsibility to prepare the whole world in its processes of globalisation and to renew the dignity of theological anthropology for the occupation of a more "personal" reformation of institutionalised Christianity that is post-Catholic and post-Protestant.

The Gifford lectures of John Macmurray (1891–1976), *The Self as Agent* and *Persons in Relation*, have profoundly

36. Michael Polanyi, *The Tacit Dimension* (New York: Doubleday, 1966).

37. Kitty Muggeridge, *Gazing on Truth: Meditations on Reality* (Grand Rapids: Eerdmans, 1985).

38. Polanyi, *Study of Man*, 69.

influenced me also.[39] The rationality, freedom, and faith of the "person" have been challenging. Seeking objectivity, Macmurray adopted the concept of "the self as agent," as acting appropriately to the nature of the other, for example, mechanically with matter, biologically with life forms, and personally with other human beings. As T. F. Torrance accepted this, he developed the dictum that "the innate logic of the object studied determines how it should be known," that is, related to. Macmurray argued further to affirm that personal knowledge is only possible to an agent, never to a mere observer. He then differentiated how the conditions of knowing in science, the arts, and religion are to be distinguished.[40] Holding that personal relations are the highest and most satisfying form of relations human beings can have, Macmurray then maintains friendship to be the highest form of personal relationship. This is how I came to write my book on prayer, *The Transforming Friendship*.[41] Friends associate for the sole purpose of being together, accepting each other unconditionally, mutually, and freely. Most profoundly we share this with God. It is also how a

39. John Macmurray, *The Self as Agent* (Atlantic Highlands, NJ: Humanities Press, 1978); *Persons in Relation* (Atlantic Highlands, NJ: Humanities Press, 1961).

40. John Macmurray, *Religion, Art and Science* (Liverpool: Liverpool University Press, 1961).

41. James M. Houston, *The Transforming Friendship: A Guide to Prayer* (Vancouver: Regent College Publishing, 2010).

child enters the world on its mother's breast, and how we care for our aging parents at the end of life.

But the flaw in Macmurray's philosophy was how he wanted to radically reshape the "religious dimension of reality," disenchanted as he was with his fundamentalist upbringing. His notion of personal freedom was not safe-guarded by Augustine's "love and do what you want," for *eros* is not *agapē*. He and his spouse engaged in spousal swapping, which he regretted later in his life.

Influenced by Macmurray, Tony Blair gave British socialism a more human face, which quietly undermined the traditional socialist ideology of the trade unions Mrs. Thatcher had confronted more violently.[42] But it was Em-manuel Mounier (1903–50) in France that had the broad-est vision for France, and indeed for the twentieth century, of a new "personal culture" and even the anticipation of a new global renaissance.[43] It was a pedagogy in revolt against universities as being afflicted with the terrible dis-ease of being impersonal. As a man of dialogue, he was not there to master but to communicate. So he confesses, "I am not much of a philosopher: does a philosopher con-sider a friendship more precious than a thesis?"[44] Yet how-

42. A. R. C. Duncan, *John Macmurray Studies: On the Nature of Per-sons* (New York: Peter Lang, 1990).

43. Emmanuel Mounier, *Personalism,* trans. Philip Mairet (London: Routledge, 1952).

44. Eileen Cantin, *Mounier: A Personalist View of History* (New York: Paulist Press, 1973), 29.

ever selfless and untiring—and full of remarkably wise aphorisms—he was in his national campaign in the pursuit of the personal, like Macmurray he turned against the source of transcendence in religion and instead sought it in the abstract sources of social relationship with an echo of Marxism and Socialism in his premises. Tragically, he died exhausted at only forty-five in 1950.[45]

Ricoeur's Critique of Kant

Fourth and finally, Mournier's long-time friend Paul Ricoeur (1913–2005) appreciated Mounier's "personal intention," but as a Christian and also a great philosopher—perhaps the most brilliant of the twentieth century—Ricoeur transcended all these earlier attempts to pursue the personal.[46] Ricoeur died at the ripe old age of ninety-two in 2005. His Gifford lectures in 1986 followed on Macmurray's earlier Gifford lectures, which he titled *On Selfhood: The Question of Personal Identity*. Later they were published and translated as *Oneself as Another*.[47] He begins by positing the question, Who is this "I" (or French "*Soi*") that thinks like the Enlightenment philosophers,

45. See the critical essay by Paul Ricoeur, "Emmanuel Mounier: A Personalist Philosopher," in *History and Truth* (Evanston, IL: Northwestern University Press, 2007), 133–64.

46. Paul Ricoeur, "The Image of God and the Epic of Man," in *History and Truth*, 110–28.

47. Paul Ricoeur, *Oneself as Another*, trans. Kathleen Blamey (Chicago: University of Chicago Press, 1994).

or indeed like his existentialist peers Sartre, Camus, Foucault, or Lacan? Secondly, he pursues the dual notions of human identity, as *ipse* ("oneself") and *idem* ("the same as"). Thirdly, how can otherness/alterity not merely be an antonym of difference, but of such intimacy that the "I" cannot be truly the self without "the other?" Profound as his development of these three pursuits are, they are grounded upon the biblical truth of the *imago dei*, of humanity made in the image of God. Quoting the church fathers, he reminds us of the words of Irenaeus: "Because of his immense love, he [God] became what we are so that he makes us what he is himself."[48] The Fathers also knew the collectivity of the one and the many, *ipse* and *idem*. We know today the broken nature of our humanity—we have private lives and public lives with their indirect economic, social, and political relationships. This dichotomy makes madness of them both, the very antithesis of biblical anthropology. Language is the mediator between the *ipse* and the *idem*. We are human because we can speak, and community is institutionally possible because we have a grammar for it.

We began this survey with Hamann's critique of Kant, and we conclude with Ricoeur's critique of Kant. In Kant's *Anthropology from a Pragmatic Point of View*, he positions a highly individualistic *ipse* as having three core passions: possession, domination, and ostentation. These passions

48. Ibid., 120.

represent, respectively, the economic sphere of having, the political sphere of power, and the cultural sphere of mutual recognition. The first relates work with ownership, the second with the governing and the governed, and the third with the power of value. Ricoeur interprets the tower of Babel as the personal/communal breakdown resulting from the loss of common language. It wrecks also the role of possession, as capital/money now exists in the abstract. Power is fundamental to political order and the unfolding of history, but as the unrighteous kings of the Old Testament demonstrate, it destroys the mandate of loving the neighbour and alienates community. Recognition and esteem of the other, the third quality that builds up culture, is also destroyed in the image of the impersonal—a work of art, a piece of literature, a poem: creative, yet a muted, often distorted expression of the *imago dei*. In such a sweep, Ricoeur would pursue the personal as broadly as his friend Mounier tried, but with far more biblical realism.

In a Socratic essay titled "The Socius and the Neighbour," Ricoeur observes that sociology as a science of human relationships in organized groups ironically has no sociology for the neighbour. Providing biblical sustenance for the category of the person, Ricoeur notes the parable of Jesus that begins, "A certain man going from Jerusalem to Jericho who fell among thieves who stripped him and wounded him." The questioner had asked a theoretical sociological question: "Who is my neighbour?" Jesus' response is that I do not *have* a neighbour; I *am* a neighbour. The "Person" in the narrative of the Good Samaritan particularises one's situation with one's neighbour, preventing them from reducing them to abstract moral categories.[49] After this meditation on "embracing the personal in Christian education," we might meet a student tomorrow morning, and we will do what the immediate situation challenges us to do. It is an awakening of conscience. It is a change of identity from being an individual to being "in Christ." It is always seeing our life within history, within personal narrative, not in abstractions and reductions.

Conclusion

A new moment is now upon us, which we can only leave to our pupils to begin to address. For beyond what Jacques Ellul could have anticipated of the technological society, there is now the further "electronic revolution" of cyberspace with its intensification of communicability. A new generation of philosophers of cyberspace like Albert Borgmann are needed to explore the new challenges.[50] Yet

49. Paul Ricoeur, "The Socius and the Neighbor," in *History and Truth*, 98–109.

50. See three Laing lectures by Albert Borgmann, "Grace and Cyberspace," *Crux*, vol. 47 (Winter 2011): 4–12; "Pointless Perfection and Blessed Burdens," ibid., 20–28; and "Matter and Spirit in an Age of Science and Technology," ibid., 36–44.

as my colleague Craig Gay has pointed out, Kierkegaard was already vigilant about the need to balance possibility with actuality, of being creaturely within creation[51] as a personal human being, which Facebook and all other new devices will continue to distort in presenting pseudo-forms of reality. But this is beyond our historical survey, projecting into the future. What is imperative for the future of Christian higher education is that we maintain the central importance of biblical anthropology, that being created in the image of God is both our origin and our destiny. Nothing we can teach and exemplify is more important than that. For embracing the personal implies that we reject reductionism in all its forms.

51. Craig Gay, *The Way of the (Modern) World: Or, Why It's Tempting to Live As If God Doesn't Exist* (Grand Rapids: Eerdmans, 1998), 13–15.

Printed in the USA
CPSIA information can be obtained
at www.ICGtesting.com
LVHW040800200823
755726LV00006B/145

9 781573 834551